Real-World Theology

Theology

Trusting God in Everyday Life

Patrick Slyman

Real-World Theology
Copyright © 2023 Patrick Slyman
All rights reserved.

Published by:

Kress Biblical Resources

www.kressbiblical.com

Unless otherwise indicated, all scripture quotations are from the New American Standard Bible® (NASB), Copyright © 1960, 1962, 1963, 1968, 1971, 1972, 1973,1975, 1977, 1995 by The Lockman Foundation. Used by permission. www.Lockman.org

Cover Design: Abi McKinney

ISBN: 978-1-934952-79-5

DEDICATION

TO

My always supportive wife who has tirelessly served alongside me in the ministry, freeing me to study, preach, and write for the glory of our Savior.

Contents

Contents

ACKNOWLEDGMENTS

I am thankful for Jack Gamble-Smith who encouraged me to put pen to paper. I am also appreciative for those who played a part in this work: Kevin Brown, Sandi Dooling, Katie Drumm, Jack Gamble-Smith, Abi McKinney, and Sarah Slyman.

INTRODUCTION
CAN A BOOK ABOUT THEOLOGY BE FOR ME?

I know what you were thinking when you saw this book: *I've never attended seminary, nor do I plan to do so. I'm not a theologian or a seminary professor. Why would I want to read a book about theology?*

It's a common misconception of our day: Theology is only for the seminary student or scholar, the pastor or teacher, not the "normal" Christian or "everyman" in the pew.

For many, theology is an off-putting word, invoking thoughts of doctrinal debates over irrelevant topics, hard-to-pronounce words with hard-to-understand meanings, and dry, cold, boring discussions that have no bearing on life in the real-world.

But that is **not** true theology. Formal intellectualism, perhaps. Dry scholasticism, maybe. But not theology as God intended.

Theology, when done right, is the farthest thing from dull or irrelevant because theology is about God—His nature, His attributes, and His ways. That is what theology means: the study of God. And God is certainly not boring. He is the infinitely fascinating Creator. He is nowhere near irrelevant, for He has everything to do with the world in which we live.

EVERYONE IS A THEOLOGIAN

Everyone, in one way or another, is a theologian—because everyone has some idea about God. The question is not, *Am I a theologian?* The question is, *What kind of theologian am I? Good or bad? Right or wrong? God-centered or man-centered?*

If we misunderstand who God is, we misunderstand all there is—our Creator, our world, and ourselves. Without true theology (a proper view of God), we are blind men groping in the dark, unable to see where we are going, trying to make sense of things only spiritually discerned. We need theology. It is the lamp that guides our path (Psalm 119:105), the mirror that reveals who we are (James 1:23), the sword that cuts to the deepest recesses of our proud heart (Hebrews 4:12), the spiritual balm that heals our soul in a sin-wrecked world (Psalm 19:7), the medicine that promotes healthy lives in a godless age (Titus 2:1), the Word that equips for every good work (2 Timothy 3:17), and the only foundation for true worship (John 4:24).

What else is there?

THEOLOGY IN THE REAL WORLD

A.W. Tozer is right: "What comes into our minds when we think about God is the most important thing about us."[1] Our view of God (our theology) is the fountain of our life. It's the cypher by which we interpret reality, the lens through which we see ourselves and our world, and the well we draw from when our energy is sapped and our struggles mount. It's where we go to find answers

---

[1] A.W. Tozer, *Knowledge of the Holy* (Lincoln: Back to the Bible Broadcast, 1971), 7.

that are beyond our pay grade. Far from irrelevant, our theology affects every part of our life.

It is no wonder the Bible is 40% narrative. It shows that God is not cold and aloof, but alive and active, involved in the everyday issues of our everyday lives. Much of Scripture is "storied theology"[2]—a God-centered (Isaiah 43:7, 21; 48:11) account about His ways, attributes, designs, and decisions playing out in the lives of real people, living in the real world, facing real problems, and seeking real answers.

True theology is real-world theology.

ONE FAMILY, FOUR DAYS

That is why this book, a theology book, focuses on John 11—a story of one family's life over the course of four days. Four days filled with real and raw emotion. Four days of unanswered prayer and confusion, death and mourning, sorrow and pain. Four days of real people asking real questions, needing real answers. Four days of real-world theology.

Read the story below.

Now a certain man was sick, Lazarus of Bethany, the village of Mary and her sister Martha. It was the Mary who anointed the Lord with ointment, and wiped His feet with her hair, whose brother Lazarus was sick. So the sisters sent word to Him, saying, "Lord, behold, he whom You love is sick."

But when Jesus heard this, He said, "This sickness is not to end in death, but for the glory of God, so that the Son of God may be glorified by it." Now Jesus

---

[2] Jeannine K. Brown, *The Gospels as Stories* (Grand Rapids: Baker Academic, 2020), 148.

loved Martha and her sister and Lazarus. So when He heard that he was sick, He then stayed two days longer in the place where He was.

Then after this He said to the disciples, "Let us go to Judea again." The disciples said to Him, "Rabbi, the Jews were just now seeking to stone You, and are You going there again?" Jesus answered, "Are there not twelve hours in the day? If anyone walks in the day, he does not stumble, because he sees the light of this world. But if anyone walks in the night, he stumbles, because the light is not in him." This He said, and after that He said to them, "Our friend Lazarus has fallen asleep; but I go, so that I may awaken him out of sleep." The disciples then said to Him, "Lord, if he has fallen asleep, he will recover." Now Jesus had spoken of his death, but they thought that He was speaking of literal sleep. So Jesus then said to them plainly, "Lazarus is dead, and I am glad for your sakes that I was not there, so that you may believe; but let us go to him." Therefore Thomas, who is called Didymus, said to his fellow disciples, "Let us also go, so that we may die with Him."

So when Jesus came, He found that he had already been in the tomb four days. Now Bethany was near Jerusalem, about two miles off; and many of the Jews had come to Martha and Mary, to console them concerning their brother. Martha therefore, when she heard that Jesus was coming, went to meet Him, but Mary stayed at the house. Martha then said to Jesus, "Lord, if You had been here, my brother would not have died. Even now I know that whatever You ask of God, God will give You." Jesus said to her, "Your brother will rise again." Martha said to Him, "I know that he will rise again in the resurrection on the last day." Jesus said to her, "I am the resurrection and the life; he who believes in Me will live even if he dies, and everyone who lives and believes in Me will never die. Do you believe this?" She said to Him, "Yes, Lord; I have believed that You are the Christ, the Son of God, even He who comes into the world."

When she had said this, she went away and called Mary her sister, saying secretly, "The Teacher is here and is calling for you." And when she heard it, she got up quickly and was coming to Him.

Now Jesus had not yet come into the village, but was still in the place where Martha met Him. Then the Jews who were with her in the house, and consoling her, when they saw that Mary got up quickly and went out, they followed her, supposing that she was going to the tomb to weep there. Therefore, when Mary came where Jesus was, she saw Him, and fell at His feet, saying to Him, "Lord, if You had been here, my brother would not have died." When Jesus therefore saw her weeping, and the Jews who came with her also weeping, He was deeply moved in spirit and was troubled, and said, "Where have you laid him?" They said to Him, "Lord, come and see." Jesus wept. So the Jews were saying, "See how He loved him!" But some of them said, "Could not this man, who opened the eyes of the blind man, have kept this man also from dying?"

So Jesus, again being deeply moved within, came to the tomb. Now it was a cave, and a stone was lying against it. Jesus said, "Remove the stone." Martha, the sister of the deceased, said to Him, "Lord, by this time there will be a stench, for he has been dead four days." Jesus said to her, "Did I not say to you that if you believe, you will see the glory of God?" So they removed the stone. Then Jesus raised His eyes, and said, "Father, I thank You that You have heard Me. I knew that You always hear Me; but because of the people standing around I said it, so that they may believe that You sent Me." When He had said these things, He cried out with a loud voice, "Lazarus, come forth." The man who had died came forth, bound hand and foot with wrappings, and his face was wrapped around with a cloth. Jesus said to them, "Unbind him, and let him go."

Therefore many of the Jews who came to Mary, and saw what He had done, believed in Him. But some of them went to the Pharisees and told them the things which Jesus had done.

Therefore the chief priests and the Pharisees convened a council, and were saying, "What are we doing? For this man is performing many signs. If we let Him go on like this, all men will believe in Him, and the Romans will come and take away both our place and our nation." But one of them, Caiaphas, who was high priest that year, said to them, "You know nothing at all, nor do you take into account that it is expedient for you that one man die for the people, and that the whole nation not perish." Now he did not say this on his own initiative, but being high priest that year, he prophesied that Jesus was going to die for the nation, and not for the nation only, but in order that He might also gather together into one the children of God who are scattered abroad. So from that day on they planned together to kill Him. (John 11:1-53)

13

A STORY IS WORTH A THOUSAND WORDS

Dramatic, isn't it? But more than dramatic, it's theological. It's a story primarily about who God is and how God works—that He is:

- The merciful God who does not always answer prayer the way we want (vv. 1-6)
- The mighty God who determines every man's death (vv. 7-16)
- The all-wise God who confounds His followers (vv. 17-22)
- The loving God who trembles within His soul (vv. 33-38)
- The gracious God who promises future hope (vv. 23-27, 40-44)
- The saving God whom sinners reject (vv. 45-46)
- The sovereign God who rules all evil (vv. 47-53)

It's one thing to read, in abstract principle, who God is—merciful, mighty, wise, loving, gracious, saving, sovereign—but it's entirely different to see those attributes in real-time and real-life. A story is worth a thousand words, a million abstract principles.

Biblical narrative shows us, in living-color, that the past experiences of others are the very issues we face today, but (and this is key) from a God-centered (i.e., theological) point of view. True theology reminds us that our life goes far beyond us, that our story is primarily God's story. True theology is real-world theology.

CREATED TO BE A THEOLOGIAN

Theology **is** for everyone—from the academic elite to the laymen in the pew—because theology is what we do every day, whether we are aware of it or not. Who we believe God to be influences every facet of our life. And the God described in John 11 is awesome, yet caring; powerful, yet loving; transcendent, yet imminent; wise, yet confounding—all at the same time, and all for the good of His people.

God created us to be theologians, good theologians, who believe, love, obey, and worship Him with all our being (Deuteronomy 6:5). This is real-world theology; this is the theologian we all must strive to become.

1

THE MERCIFUL GOD OF UNANSWERED PRAYER (PT. 1)

Now a certain man was sick, Lazarus of Bethany, the village of Mary and her sister Martha. It was the Mary who anointed the Lord with ointment, and wiped His feet with her hair, whose brother Lazarus was sick. So the sisters sent word to Him, saying, "Lord, behold, he whom You love is sick." But when Jesus heard this...He then stayed two days longer in the place where He was. (John 11:1-3, 6)

Prayer is utterly profound—the creature piercing heaven with his words.[3] Prayer is a Gospel privilege: Now reconciled to God, clothed in the righteousness of Jesus, we have the freedom to approach our sovereign Savior's throne of grace; not in cowering fear, but with bold confidence (Hebrews 4:16). Prayer is a refuge—the weak and lowly coming to the Rock of our salvation (Psalm 62:2), casting all our cares upon Him, knowing that He cares for us (1 Peter 5:7). Prayer is a reminder of God's immanence and care: "The righteous cry, and LORD hears" (Psalm 34:17). The wonder of that verse never ceases to amaze me.

---

[3] This imagery is taken from *Piercing Heaven: Prayers of the Puritans*, ed. Robert Elmer (Bellingham: Lexham Press, 2019).

And yet, what do we often experience in the Christian life? Unanswered prayer, when heaven's access seems barred to God's children. Every believer has experienced God's *no* to their most sincere requests. Abraham, singled out to receive God's covenant, asked for Sodom and Gomorrah to be spared, and yet God sent fire from heaven to destroy the cities (Genesis 18-19). David, a man after God's own heart, prayed for his son to live, and still God brought death to the family (2 Samuel 12:14-31). Paul, that specially called Apostle, pleaded for his thorn in the flesh to be removed, but God let it remain (2 Corinthians 12:7-9).

Unanswered prayer is an everyday part of the Christian life. We echo the psalmist, "O my God, I cry by day, but You do not answer" (Psalm 22:2). There are nights when, through our tears, we ask, *Where are you, God?* (Psalm 42:3) and mornings when we wonder if the darkness of unanswered prayer will ever lift.

A STORY ABOUT UNANSWERED PRAYER

Why does God say *no* to our most sincere requests, greatest hopes, and most heartfelt desires? Why does He not open heaven's storehouse of grace when we knock, and plead, and beg?

These are the real-world questions that begin the story in John 11. Mary and Martha plead with Jesus to heal Lazarus, only to hear Him say *no*. They ask for their brother to live, only to see him die. They appeal for Jesus to come to their home quickly, only to wait in expectation for days. And yet, as the story progresses, Jesus' *no* is shown to be what was best for this family. His silence was for their good—a principle that remains true for every Christian who hears *no* from God.

Real-world theology grasps unanswered prayer.

TWO SISTERS PRAY

The story opens with these words, "Now a certain man was sick, Lazarus of Bethany" (John 11:1). This was no ordinary sickness.

17

"Sick" (*astheneo*) described a condition that utterly devastated the body. John has used this word before to describe a nobleman's son who was "**sick**... to the point of death" (John 4:46, emphasis mine) and a lame man who was "**ill** for thirty-eight years" (John 5:5, emphasis mine). Lazarus had succumbed to sickness of the severest sort. Debilitating. Deadly. Terminal. And his sisters knew his prognosis. Without supernatural intervention, their brother would die.

OF COURSE LAZARUS WILL BE HEALED...RIGHT?

If you did not already know this story, every indication leads you to believe that Jesus will answer the sisters' prayer.

Hope filled Mary and Martha as this chapter opens. Though their request for healing was left unexpressed, it was certainly implied—and expected.

First, they knew Jesus' power—He was the one who had, for the past three years, shown His mastery over every disease. Whether leprosy, paralysis, blindness, or a withered hand, there was no ailment outside Jesus' healing touch. Think of Mark 6:56, "Wherever He entered villages, or cities, or countryside, they were laying the sick in the market places, and imploring Him that they might just touch the fringe of His cloak; and as many as touched it were being cured."

Second, they knew Jesus' special love for Lazarus— which is why the sisters did not use Lazarus' name in their prayer. Lazarus was simply, "he whom You love" (John 11:3), one of only two people in John's Gospel referred to in this way (John 19:26). And to deepen Jesus' affection for Lazarus even further, John chose this moment to describe Jesus' love for the first time in his Gospel. In John 3, we were told that the Father loved the world (John 3:16). In John 5, the Father loved the Son (John 5:20). In John 8, people loved Jesus (John 8:42). And yet, up to this point in John's Gospel, there has been no mention of Jesus' love for others. Of course Jesus loved people, but it has only been an implied love. But now, as Lazarus grew ill, Jesus' love becomes explicit.

Third, they knew Jesus' mercy. He had healed thousands over the past three years, many of whom Jesus did not personally know. But Jesus knew Lazarus. And He knew him well.

Fourth, whenever we read the word "sick" throughout the Gospels, it is always in a healing context. To the nobleman, whose son was "sick...to the point of death...Jesus said to him, 'Go; your son lives'" (John 4:50). To the man lame for 38 years, "Jesus said to him, 'Get up, pick up your pallet and walk'" (John 5:8).

Jesus will surely heal our brother whom He loves, was what the sisters thought. *How could Lazarus be the one exception to Jesus' healing ministry?* And so, they hope. And pray. And plead. And wait.

THE SAVIOR DELAYS

And yet what did Jesus do? How did He answer Mary and Martha's intercession for their brother? He said, *no.* He chose **not** to speak a word of healing from a distance as He did for the nobleman's son (John 4:50). He decided **not** to transport Himself through time and space, like He did when He calmed the storm (John 6:21). He even refused to travel with the messengers back to Bethany. He delayed. Waited. Stayed. For four long days.[4] "So when He heard that he was sick, He stayed two days longer in the place where He was" (John 11:6).

---

[4] One day for the messengers to give Jesus the news. Two days, as Jesus stayed away. And a fourth day for Jesus to arrive at Mary and Martha's home.

Think of the agony Mary and Martha must have experienced. Four days of sorrow. Four days of funeral preparations. Four days of tears. Four days of questioning Jesus' love for them.

WHY *NO*, LORD?

Why did you not answer my prayer, Lord? Why are you not easing my pain? Why are you not taking away my sorrow? I've asked with tears. I've asked with hope. I've asked in faith. I know You have the power to grant my request. I know You love me. So, why have You not moved? Why have You not worked?

These are real-world questions we've all asked. And often our search for answers comes up dry. We look for signs only to be disappointed. We seek counsel from friends. Each time forgetting that answers to those questions have already been given.

Jesus had not left Mary and Martha in the dark. He sent messengers back with an important message—an explanation for why He chose to not heal Lazarus, why He did not grant the sisters' request, why He let Lazarus die.

And the reasons Jesus gave these sisters are the same reasons He does not answer many of our prayers today—reasons we will explore in the next chapter.

2

THE MERCIFUL GOD OF UNANSWERED PRAYER (PT. 2)

But when Jesus heard this, He said, "This sickness is not to end in death, but for the glory of God, so that the Son of God may be glorified by it." Now Jesus loved Martha and her sister and Lazarus. So when He heard that he was sick, He then stayed two days longer in the place where He was. (John 11:4-6)

In chapter 1, we saw a real-world example of God choosing to **not** answer a sincere request from those whom He loves.

This was how John 11 began. Jesus stayed away from Bethany for four long days as Lazarus, the one whom He loved (11:3), died. He said *no* to the urgent calls of Mary and Martha to come to them. You can hear the sorrow in their words: "Lord, if you had been here" (11:21). Jesus had healed so many others, even strangers, and from afar. And yet, He does not heal this beloved friend. Instead, He lets Lazarus die and the sisters sorrow.

Is this not how our Savior often answers our prayers? We cry out with tears, knowing His love for us, but He doesn't move when we plead. The silence seems to whisper, *Is He really there? Does He even care?*

Why does God sometimes say *no* to our most earnest prayers? Let's resume the story to find out.

FOR GOD'S GLORY

First, Jesus refused to answer the sisters' request because that was what would most exalt His Father's glory. "For the glory of God" (John 11:4) was Jesus' reason.[5] God being glorified was most important to Jesus (John 12:28)—and it is what must be most important to us. Why? Because God's glory is always for our best. His glory is always for our joy. His glory is our greatest good. And thus, we must be satisfied with God's *no*, if that is how He sees fit to best put His glory on display.

The overarching purpose of all that God does—including His *no* to many of our most heartfelt prayers—is the praise of His glorious name (Isaiah 48:11).[6] God will not grant our prayers if they detract from His glory in any way.

Jesus delayed so that His Father might receive highest praise. He stayed away so that God's mercy and grace would shine most brightly. Jesus let Lazarus die because it was best for these sisters. In the words of one author, "God's glory does not consist in sparing the faithful life's difficulties."[7] Quite often, God's glory only comes through life's sorrows (Psalm 30:5).

---

[5] "For the glory of God" was the same answer Jesus gave His Apostles in John 9:4, when asked why a man was born blind. Surely the man's parents asked for a healthy baby boy. And surely, once they realized their son could not see, they prayed for him to be given sight. But to each of those prayers, God answered no. Why? Why did God allow the boy's blindness? Why did He wait decades before giving him his sight? Why did He delay in answering the parents' prayers? Here is Jesus' answer, "It was so that the works of God might be displayed in him" (John 9:3). The man's blindness was for his good, because his blindness would one day become a vehicle for him to bring glory to his God—glory God would receive, throughout all eternity, through this man's salvation (John 9:35-38).

[6] See: Jonathan Edwards, *The End for Which God Created the World: Updated to Modern English*, ed. Jason Dollar (Westbow Press, 2018).

[7] Ernst Haenchen, as cited in Leon Morris, *The Gospel According to John*, NICNT (Grand Rapids: Eerdman's Publishing, 1995) 478.

WE NEED HIS *NO*

A second reason Jesus did not answer Mary and Martha's request was because He saw these sisters' greater need. More than a healer, they needed a Savior. By saying *no* to Mary and Martha, "Jesus began a chain of events that would lead in time to the cross."[8] This is why Jesus adds, "so that the Son of God may be glorified" (John 11:4)— a reference to His sacrificial and atoning death.

Think of John 12:23: "Jesus answered...'The hour has come for the Son of Man **to be glorified**'" (John 12:23, emphasis mine). What hour of glorification was Jesus referring to? It was the time of His death, which Jesus makes clear in the next verse, when He compared Himself to a grain of wheat that must be buried in the ground (John 12:24). The hour of the Son's death was the hour of the Son's glory. In John 17:1, Jesus made this same connection between His death and His glory: "Jesus...lifting up His eyes to heaven... said, 'Father, the hour has come; **glorify Your Son**, that the Son may glorify You'" (John 17:1, emphasis mine). The glory of Christ necessitated the cross of Christ.

Jesus delayed His trip to Bethany to set the stage for the very miracle that would seal His death sentence. Jesus let Lazarus die to give the mourners time to gather in great number at the sisters' home. He bided His time to ensure a large stone would lock the tomb's entrance, the very symbol of death's finality. He waited four days to coincide with the cultural timestamp of death's permanence.[9] All setting the stage for the most remarkable, glorious, and climatic

---

[8] Leon Morris, *Reflections on the Gospel of John* (Hendrikson Publishers, Peabody, 2000), 404.

[9] We will further explore this four-day interval in chapter 4. But for now, the words of one rabbi will suffice, "For three days the soul hovers over the body, intending to re-enter it, but as soon as it sees its appearance change [i.e., day four], it departs." As quoted in Andreas J. Kostenberger, "John" in *Zondervan Illustrated Bible Backgrounds Commentary*, ed. Clinton E. Arnold (Grand Rapids: Zondervan, 2002), 109.

miracle Jesus would perform in His lifetime—raising Lazarus from the dead.

Why? **So that** word would get back to the religious leaders that Jesus did what no mere mortal could do: reach into Sheol, the realm that belonged to God alone, and snatch life from the claws of death (Psalm 68:20). **So that** the Sanhedrin would finally meet and officially sign His death sentence. **So that** He would be raised on a cross, which is exactly how the story of Lazarus ends: "Therefore the chief priests convened a council...So from that day they planned to kill Him" (John 11:47, 53).

WISDOM, GRACE, AND PROVIDENCE

Here is the wisdom of Christ in unanswered prayer: He sees what we do not see and He knows what we need most. Though His delay meant temporary pain for the sisters, it also meant salvation for their souls. The sisters wanted Lazarus to live, but Jesus knew they needed **Him** to die.

Here is the grace of Christ in unanswered prayer: though His *no* may bring us extreme sorrow, it is always with our eternal joy in mind. Though the sisters did not know it, they needed Jesus to say *no* to their request—as, so often, do we.

Here is the providence of God in unanswered prayer: the Lord only says *no* if it will conform us into the image of His Son. His *no* is His way of sanctifying His children. In the words of J.I. Packer,

> Perhaps he means to strengthen us in patience...compassion, humility or meekness...Perhaps he has new lessons in self-denial and self-distrust to teach us. Perhaps he wishes to break us of complacency or undetected forms of pride and conceit. Perhaps His purpose is simply to draw us closer to himself...Or

perhaps God is preparing us for forms of service of which at present we have no inkling.[10]

The Lord's *no*, is always His *yes* to our greater need.

BECAUSE HE LOVES

A third reason Jesus said *no* to Mary and Martha is because He loved them.

This seems counterintuitive, doesn't it? So often we interpret the Lord's *no* as a lack of love, not proof of it. But notice verse 5: Jesus said *no*, **because** He loved: "Now Jesus **loved** Martha and her sister and Lazarus" (John 11:5, emphasis mine). On the surface, verse 5 is an unnecessary editorial note because John has already told us that Jesus loved this family in verse 3. And yet, for some reason, John felt the need to remind his readers of Jesus' love for them.

But more than a reminder, verse 5 actually deepens Jesus' love for this family. First, John specified that Jesus loved each family member individually; He did not only love Lazarus, "Jesus loved Martha and her sister" (John 11:5). Second, John used a different, more intense word for love in verse 5. In verse 3, Jesus loved Lazarus with a *phileo* love, a kind of brotherly love. But in verse 5, Jesus loved each member of this family with an *agapao* love—the most personal and profound type of love (John 3:16, 19, 35; 8:42; 10:17). Third, John put the verb "love" in the imperfect tense, indicating that Jesus' love for this family was a dependable, never-failing love.

This leads to several questions: *Why did John feel the need to remind us of Jesus' love for this family? Why specifically mention Jesus' love for each member of the family? Why deepen Jesus' love for them? Why emphasize the*

---

[10] J.I. Packer, *Knowing God* (Intervarsity: Downers Grove: 1993), 91.

dependable, never-failing nature of Jesus' love? Answer: Because John knew, once we read that Jesus did not heal Lazarus in verse 6, we would doubt His love for Mary, Martha, and Lazarus. We would question it.

"So when He heard that he was sick, He then stayed two days longer in the place where He was" (John 11:6). Without a reminder of Jesus' reliable, never-failing, deepest kind of affection for each member of this family, Jesus' response seems callous, heartless, and cold.

Put yourself in Mary and Martha's shoes. When the messengers came back—without Jesus—would you have felt loved by Jesus? "It would have felt like betrayal."[11] In fact, isn't that what we hear the sisters say when Jesus arrived, "Lord, if You had been here, my brother would not have died" (John 11:21). Where were you, Jesus? Why weren't you here when we needed You most? We thought You loved us? We thought You cared?

But verse 5 is clear. Jesus waited because He loved. Unbeknownst to Martha and Mary, it would have been unloving for Jesus to give them what they asked. And so it is each time the Lord says no to us—it would be unloving for Him to say yes.

NO GOOD THING WILL HE WITHHOLD

When we pray, we want Jesus to act immediately, don't we? We want Him to relieve our pain and take away our sorrow. Instantly! We want answers now, not later. We want relief today, not tomorrow. Waiting is not our strong suit, especially in our "give-it-to-me-now" culture. And yet our Lord, because of His great love for us, often will not give us what we want. Like a caring father who refuses to withhold pain from his child when that pain is for the child's

---

[11] Matt Carter and Josh Wredberg, *Christ-Centered Exposition: Exalting Jesus in John* (Holman: Nashville, 2017), 228.

good, so too, our loving Savior refuses to answer our prayers when they are too shortsighted for our own good.

Every time the Lord answers no to our prayers, He fulfills Psalm 84:11, "No good thing does He withhold from those who walk uprightly." (Psalm 84:11). Mary, Martha, and Lazarus were an upright family (John 12:1-3). Faith filled their home (John 11:27, 32). Jesus did not delay because the sisters were in sin. He said no because it was for their benefit.[12]

OUR PRAYERS, GOD'S PROMISE

Though we may never know the specifics of why the Lord does not grant many of our requests, real-world theology believes that every time God says no, He is not keeping anything good from us, but is bestowing great love upon us.

We pray, not to change the mind of God, but to cast our cares upon Him. We pray, not to inform Him of what He does not already know, but to rest our worries on His perfect wisdom. We pray because He loves us, works for us, and promises never to withhold anything good from us. His *no* is actually His *yes*—yes to what is better than what we even think to ask for.

---

[12] "Christ knows best at what time to do anything for His people....The children of God must constantly school their minds to learn the great lesson now before us. Nothing so helps us to bear patiently the trials of life as an abiding conviction of the perfect wisdom by which everything around us is managed. Let us try to believe not only that all that happens to us is well done, but that it is done in the best manner, by the right instrument, and at the right time. We are all naturally impatient in the day of trial...We forget that Christ is too wise a Physician to make any mistakes....Let us believe that He by whom all things were made at first is He who is managing with all perfect wisdom. The affairs of kingdoms, families, and private individuals are all... overruled by Him. He chooses all the portions of His people. When we are sick, it is because He knows it to be for our good; when He delays coming to help us, it is for some wise reason. The hand that was nailed to the cross is too wise and loving to smite without a needs-be, or to keep us waiting for relief without a cause." J.C. Ryle, "St. John," *Expository Thoughts on the Gospels*, (New York: Robert Carter and Brothers, 1878), 231.

3
THE POWERFUL GOD WHO ORDAINS OUR DEATH

Then after this He said to the disciples, "Let us go to Judea again." The disciples said to Him, "Rabbi, the Jews were just now seeking to stone You, and are You going there again?" Jesus answered, "Are there not twelve hours in the day? If anyone walks in the day, he does not stumble, because he sees the light of this world. But if anyone walks in the night, he stumbles, because the light is not in him." This He said, and after that He said to them, "Our friend Lazarus has fallen asleep; but I go, so that I may awaken him out of sleep." The disciples then said to Him, "Lord, if he has fallen asleep, he will recover." Now Jesus had spoken of his death, but they thought that He was speaking of literal sleep. So Jesus then said to them plainly, "Lazarus is dead, and I am glad for your sakes that I was not there, so that you may believe; but let us go to him." Therefore Thomas, who is called Didymus, said to his fellow disciples, "Let us also go, so that we may die with Him." (John 11:7-16)

Thanatophobia is the term for the fear of death. It's the fear of the unknown afterlife, the anxiety of watching a loved one suffer, the dread of knowing your days have reached their end. For many, death is a frightening reality. It wields a big stick and threatens great loss.

Fifty-six million people die every year. One hundred and fifty thousand die every day. Six thousand every hour. One hundred every minute. These numbers are too staggering to wrap our minds around. Every day, death stalks. Every hour, death strikes. Every minute, death wins. It's no wonder death has been described as "the king of terrors" (Job 18:14).

Death conquers all—"What man can live and not see death?" (Psalm 89:48).[13] Death shows no partiality: "the wise man and the fool alike die!" (Ecclesiastes 2:16). Death reveals our brevity (Psalm 103:15), exposes our weakness (Job 14:2), taunts us with its suddenness (Job 21:13), and mocks us with its power (Ecclesiastes 8:8). It strips us of our possessions and steals loved ones from our homes. Death hurts. It ruptures our body from its soul. It robs. Devours. Death is an intrusion into God's original design (Genesis 1-2).

Perhaps this anonymous author captured the power of death best with these picturesque words,

> He is a preacher of the old school, but he speaks as boldly as ever. He is not popular, though the world is his parish and he travels over every part of the globe and speaks in every language. He visits the poor; calls upon the rich and preaches to people of every religion and no religion, and the subject of his sermons is always the same. He is an eloquent preacher and he often stirs the feelings, which no other preacher can stir and brings tears to eyes that seldom weep. His arguments none are able to refute; nor is there any heart that has remained unmoved by the force of his appeals. He shatters life with his message. Most people hate him; everyone fears him. His name? Death. Every tombstone is his pulpit. Every newspaper prints his text. And one day, every one of us will be his message.[14]

Linger over that last line, "And one day, every one of us will be his message." It's chilling. And true.

---

[13] The only exception is the rapture of the church, which is an imminent event (John 14:1-3; 1 Thessalonians 4:13-18).

[14] As quoted in John MacArthur, *1 Corinthians* (Chicago: Moody Press, 1996), 441-42.

EVEN CHRISTIANS FEAR DEATH

For weeks Jesus had remained in the safety of northern Palestine, outside the reach of the Jerusalem council. This was one reason why Jesus chose not to immediately return to Judea when word came of Lazarus' sickness, even though He loved him very much. But as verse 7 opens, Jesus' travel plans have drastically changed. "Let us go to Judea," Jesus says (John 10:7).

Had the Apostles heard Jesus correctly? Judea? The den of lions where Jesus had almost been arrested and murdered on multiple occasions (John 5:18; 7:1, 30; 8:59; 10:31, 39)?

The Apostles were confused. But even more, they were fearful: "Rabbi, the Jews were just now seeking to stone You, and are You going there again?" (John 10:8). Hear the trembling in their worried words. They don't want to die, they want to live. They want to avoid the grave, not tempt their fate. Later in the story, Thomas will verbalize the Apostles' apprehension: "Let us also go, so that we may die with Him" (John 10:16). Thomas dreaded the inevitable outcome: If Jesus left for Judea, He would die—**and so would they**.

THE NEED OF OUR DAY

If there is ever a time the American church needs a real-world theology of fear and death, it is now. We need to rekindle our belief that death is **not** the "king of terrors" it postures itself to be. We need to be reminded that our goal in life is **not** to preserve our temporal existence, but to prepare ourselves for future glory. We need to accept that our calling is **not** to escape the grave, but to spread the Gospel.

We need to once again hear Jesus' words to His fearful Apostles, "Are there not twelve hours in a day? If anyone walks in the day, he does not stumble, because he sees the light of this world. But if anyone walks in the night, he stumbles" (John 11:9-10).

Jesus was drawing from the custom of the day. People traveled during the day, not the night. They wanted to see where they were going and not trip on the rocky roads or twist an ankle in the potholes along the paths. Daytime travel was even a way to mitigate the threat of bandits who often attacked the unsuspecting on the busy highways. It was a basic axiom: one traveled while it was light to ensure safety, avoid injury, and even escape death.

A simple parable, but it teaches a profound principle.

YOU WILL NOT DIE BEFORE YOUR APPOINTED TIME

The lesson is this: **You will not die before your appointed time.** Just as there are "twelve hours in a day," there is also a set number of days in your life (Psalm 139:16).

Jesus made a similar comparison in John 9:4, "We must work the works of Him who sent Me as long as it is day." **Day** is analogous to Jesus' ministry, His time on earth allotted Him by His Father, while **night** refers to Jesus' death. As Jesus put it, "Night is coming when no one can work" (John 9:4), a picture of His arrest, trial, and crucifixion—when the sun would set on His earthly life. Daylight referred to life, nighttime referred to death.

In other words: *As long as you are traveling* (living*) in the light* (the days appointed to you by God)*, you have nothing to fear; you will not stumble, you will not trip, you will not be overtaken by bandits—you will not die. Just as God has appointed twelve hours in the daytime, so too, God has assigned a certain number of days in your lifetime. Darkness* (death) *will never come early on God's calendar.* A lesson Jesus' fearful Apostles needed to grasp.

THERE IS NO "RISK" IN GOD'S SOVEREIGN DECREE

Of course, on the surface, Jesus' return to Judea looked risky—not only for Him, but also for those closest to Him. Retaliation from the religious leaders was a real possibility. But the reality of the situation was this: Jesus' hour had not yet come (John 7:30; 8:20). Jesus was traveling in the appointed daylight hours; and thus, He had nothing to fear. But this was not only true for Jesus—it was also true for His Apostles. Like Jesus, the sun was still shining upon them. Like Jesus, dusk was not yet. They, too, were living on a sovereign timetable, one where the sun never sets early.

In God's sovereign decree, there is no risk of dying before your appointed time. Every moment of every day has already been determined by God: "In Your book were written the days that were ordained for me" (Psalm 139:16). The number of your days has been decreed by the divine: "[Man's] days are determined, the number of his months is with You; and his limits You have set so that he cannot pass" (Job 14:5).

FREED TO BE FAITHFUL

Now do not take from this principle a freedom to be reckless about your life, or foolish about your decisions. Not dying before your appointed time does not give a free pass to play Frogger in the road. But it does bring freedom—freedom to live in obedience to Christ without fearing our life could ever be cut short. That is why Jesus called His Apostles to walk by "the light of the world" (John 11:9) as He ended His analogy. A play on words for sure, since Jesus had recently used that exact phrase to describe Himself: "I am the light of the world" (John 8:12). In other words, the sovereignly determined sunlight of your earthly days is what frees you to walk in obedience to the light of Christ.

For the Apostles, that meant traveling with Jesus to Judea, knowing the deadly threats that awaited Him—and them. For us, it means something different, but the same principle applies: We walk in Christ's light as long as it is day. We follow His commands as long as we have life. We pursue His glory—no matter the earthly threat, or the most doomsday prediction—assured that every one of our moments has been written in a book, secured by the power of our Savior.

IS IT POSSIBLE TO MOVE FROM FEAR TO FAITH?

But in a day when we are told that death is the worst thing that could happen to us, and life is to be preserved at all costs, is fearless living even possible? Can we (personally) buck the trend, and move from dreading death to living in the light of Christ? The answer is *yes*—and Thomas is case in point. The same fearful Apostle, singled out in verse 16, is the very disciple John quoted at the end of his Gospel: "Thomas...said to Him, 'My Lord and my God'" (John 20:28).

Thomas learned the lesson. He confessed Jesus to be the Lord of life, the conqueror of death, and the God who rules every grave. And thus, Thomas fearlessly preached Christ's Gospel for the next three decades, until he was speared to death by pagan priests.[15] Thomas-the-fearful became Thomas-the-faithful because he believed the sun would not set one moment sooner than God had ordained.

Is this not what our world needs to see? Today? From us? Fearless Christians confessing Jesus to be the Lord of life—not trying to escape the grave, but living for the Gospel—until that last God-ordained breath.

May we, too, learn Jesus' real-world theology lesson as Thomas did: We will not die before our appointed time.

---

[15] John Foxe, *Foxe's Christian Martyrs of the World* (Chicago: Moody Press, n.d.), 34.

4

THE ALL-WISE GOD WHO CONFOUNDS
HIS FOLLOWERS (PT. 1)

So when Jesus came, He found that he had already been in the tomb four days. Now Bethany was near Jerusalem, about two miles off; and many of the Jews had come to Martha and Mary, to console them concerning their brother. Martha therefore, when she heard that Jesus was coming, went to meet Him, but Mary stayed at the house. Martha then said to Jesus, "Lord, if You had been here, my brother would not have died. Even now I know that whatever You ask of God, God will give You." (John 11:17-22)

"Oh, the depth of the riches both of the wisdom and knowledge of God! How unsearchable are His judgments and unfathomable His ways! For WHO HAS KNOWN THE MIND OF THE LORD, OR WHO BECAME HIS COUNSELOR?...For from Him and through Him and to Him are all things. To Him be the glory forever. Amen" (Romans 11:33- 34, 36).

That profound doxology ends the first section of Romans, calling us to our knees in worship and praise, exalting the Lord for His majestic knowledge, transcendent omniscience, and perfect wisdom. It's a doxology of comfort for the believer, knowing that God needs no counselor, that His judgments are always righteous, and His ways are always good.

God's wisdom is unmatched. He knows "the end from the beginning" (Isaiah 46:10). He comprehends all contingencies—not only what has happened and will happen, but what could have happened in any given scenario (Jeremiah 23:21-22). His ways are higher than our ways, His thoughts are not our thoughts (Isaiah 55:9). God's knowledge is an unplumbable mystery, a bottomless ocean, an endless queue. Unfathomable, unattainable, unsearchable—all biblical descriptions of God's mind. No wonder the psalmist declares, "Such knowledge is too wonderful for me; it is too high, I cannot attain it" (Psalm 139:6).

And yet what do we find to be true throughout the Christian life? That the infinite wisdom of our God—the wisdom that brings us so much comfort—is also the very wisdom that leaves us in a state of so much confusion. We find ourselves perplexed by the Lord's decisions, mystified by His decrees. Not doubting God, but unsettled, unnerved—wondering, asking, guessing—trying to make sense of a chaotic world that looks to be outside of its Creator's control.

The wisdom that leads us to worship is the same wisdom that leads us to wonder. Confused, we ask, *Why Lord?* A question that is often left unanswered.

CRIES OF CONFUSION

Scripture is replete with cries of confusion.

"Why do You hide Your face and consider me Your enemy?" (Job 13:24).

"Why do You stand afar off, O LORD? Why do You hide Yourself in times of trouble?" (Psalm 10:1).

"Why have You rejected me…Why do You sleep, O Lord?" (Psalm 44:2, 23).

"My God, my God, why have You forsaken me?" (Psalm 22:1).

I'm hearing these same questions today. *Why does it seem the Lord has forgotten me, even though I am seeking to be faithful? Why is there so much pain in my life? Why is there so much sorrow and hurt within my family? Why is there so much evil in this world? Why Lord, why?*

Real-world theology seeks answers to these questions.

YOU ARE NOT ALONE

If God's wisdom has ever left you stunned, groping for answers—if you have ever asked God, *why?*—you are not alone. That is the very question Mary and Martha had been asking for the past three days.

As John 11:17 opens, these two sisters were dazed and confused. Jesus' words seemed clear, "This sickness is not to end in death" (John 11:4), but there was Lazarus—dead in a tomb. Jesus' love seemed sure (John 11:3), but the messengers came back without Jesus by their side. For three days Mary and Martha felt alone, forsaken in their most desperate time of need, wondering, *Why? Why is Jesus not here? Why did He not bring the comfort we needed?* Confusion reigns. Questions fly. *Why has Jesus hidden His face from us? Why has He allowed death to win? And sorrow to reign? And tears to flow? Why Lord, why?*

CONFUSED BY DEATH

When Jesus finally arrived in Bethany, Lazarus had "already been in the tomb four days" (John 11:17), a critical time marker that explains Mary and Martha's confusion. Precise time intervals are not John's typical style. "After this" or "After these things" is how John usually progresses his story. But not here. Not now. Not when describing Lazarus' death.

There are only three places in his Gospel where John designates specific days, and each time he does, it is always for a theological purpose. The first time-stamp John includes is his description of the opening week of Jesus' messianic ministry (John 1:29, 35, 43; 2:1). The theological significance of this time marker is to present Jesus as the incarnation of the Creator (John 1:3). As the Lord who created the world in seven days, Jesus worked for seven days, ending

His week in miraculous fashion. Who is Jesus? He is the Creator who has come to bring a new creation.[16]

John's third time-stamp occurs during the final week of Jesus' life. The theological significance here is to connect Jesus' death to the Passover lamb sacrifice (John 12:1), while also showing Him to be the resurrected Son of God (John 20:1; cf. 2:20-21).

But what significance does this second time-stamp carry—the four-day period of Lazarus's death, mentioned not just once, but twice (John 11:39)? To answer this question, one needs to understand these four days of death in their cultural context.

The first-century theory was that the soul would hover over a dead body for three days. But on the fourth day, once the body began to decompose, the soul would leave. One rabbi explained it this way: "For three days the soul hovers over the body, intending to re-enter it, but as soon as it sees its appearance change, it departs."[17] Another rabbi wrote, "The full force of mourning lasts for three days. Why? Because for three days the shape of the face is recognizable."[18]

John noted this "four day" period to stress the **finality** of Lazarus' death and the **hopelessness** this family was experiencing.[19] Death had won. The king of terror reigned. The darkened tomb mocked the promise Jesus sent the sisters in verse 4, "This sickness is not to end in death." The stone that locked the front of the cave begged the question, "How could Jesus have been so wrong?"

Up to this point in John's Gospel, every word Jesus spoke had come to fruition. Every promise He made, He fulfilled. He was always "full of truth" (John 1:14)—**until now**. Jesus' promise felt hollow.

---

[16] Andreas J. Kostenberger, *The Theology of John's Gospels and Letters* (Grand Rapids: Zondervan, 2009), 349.

[17] Kostenberger, "John," 109.

[18] Ibid.

[19] The Christological significance of this four-day marker comes in v. 25, when Jesus proclaims, "I am the resurrection and the life." Jesus is death's master. Death, even in the full force of its finality, is no match for Christ's resurrecting voice. Jesus will do what He promised in John 5:28. He will call Lazarus from the grave, a foreshadowing of what He will do at the end of the age.

His pledge, presumptuous. Didn't the Old Testament warn about a prophet's unfilled promises? "The prophet who speaks a word presumptuously in My name...that prophet shall die" (Deuteronomy 18:20, 22). It's no wonder these sisters were confused.

Any hope Mary and Martha had clung to during those first three days of Lazarus' death was now gone. Day four—that dreaded, final, decisive day—had dawned. Optimism was now despair. Confidence in Christ had given way to a thousand questions for these sisters. Psalm 44:24 was no longer words on a page, it was what Mary and Martha felt—and felt deeply, "Why do You hide Your face and forget our affliction?"

"IF ONLY"

Martha's response when Jesus finally arrived is so real-to-life, "Lord, if You had been here, my brother would not have died" (John 11:21).

When confused by God's ways, isn't this how we often respond? We play the "if only" game. *If only God did it differently, then all would be better.* Sometimes we even turn the "if only" on ourselves. *If only I prayed more, or had more faith, then things would be different. If only I did something earlier or better, then all would be fine.*

"HOW LONG, O LORD?"

Martha was trying to make sense of Jesus' timing. Yes, Jesus arrived, but Martha thought it was too late. "If You had been here" was Martha's version of the many "How long, O Lord" prayers we read throughout the Scripture.

> "How long, O LORD? Will You forget me forever? How long will You hide Your face from me? How long shall I take counsel in my soul, having sorrow in my heart all the day? How long will my enemy be exalted over me?" (Psalm 13:1-2).

> "Lord, how long will You look on?" (Psalm 35:17).

"How long, O LORD, will I call for help, And You will not hear?" (Habakkuk 1:2).

Confusion about God's timing rings throughout redemptive history. Did Abraham not wonder *how long?* as he waited twenty-five years for his promised son to be born? Did Job not wonder, *how long will my sufferings last?* Did Paul not question, *how long will I endure my thorn in the flesh?* Even the martyrs under God's throne, freed from their sin-bound bodies and standing in the presence of God, ask, *how long?* "How long, O Lord, holy and true, will You refrain from judging and avenging our blood on those who dwell on the earth?" (Revelation 6:10).

Are we not asking this same question today? *How long will my illness last? How long will my loved-one suffer? How long will God wait before He avenges His holy name? How long until the Lord returns? How long before righteousness reigns? How long until judgment falls?* Confused by God's timing, we wonder, and like Martha, we often weep— surprised that the Lord has not given us the answers we seek.

WE SHOULD NOT BE SURPRISED

But should we be surprised when God's wisdom confounds us? Should we be stunned when the Lord moves in mysterious ways? Not at all!

First, God has been clear, "'My thoughts are not your thoughts, nor are your ways My ways,' declares the LORD. 'For as the heavens are higher than the earth, so are My ways higher than your ways and My thoughts than your thoughts'" (Isaiah 55:8-9). If God is going to be God, He must baffle us at times—not because of any flaw or defect in God, but because of just the opposite. Transcendence will always confound the finite. The boundless will always bewilder the created (Job 38-41).

Second, confusion is necessary because our minds are too limited to grasp all that God is doing. As John Piper notes, "God is always doing 10,000 things in your life, and you may be aware of three of them."[20] Because we are not capable of processing all the intricacies of what the Lord is doing in our lives—let alone in the lives of the eight billion people throughout the world—we are bound to be puzzled by His ways.

Third, perplexity is inevitable because we are short-sighted and impatient. Our eyes are too myopic, our thoughts too narrow. We see only today, forgetting the past and incapable of knowing the future. We want things to move quicker than they do. We want God to act sooner than when He is ready. Oh, how different is God. He is patient. He is not bound by time. "With the Lord one day is like a thousand years, and a thousand years like one day" (2 Peter 3:8). Unlike us, He sees the big picture and will not act until the perfect time.

Fourth, we will wonder because God is loving. That is the principle from John 16:12—as the hour of Jesus' death drew near, He told His Apostles, "I have many more things to say to you, but you cannot bear them now." The Lord will not inform us of His work if it is too heavy a burden for us to bear (Habakkuk 1:3). In love, the Lord only explains what we are ready to receive.[21]

Fifth, our minds must be darkened to God's ways if He is going to shine His glory most brightly. This is how the story of Lazarus ends. "Jesus said to [Martha], 'Did I not say to you that if you believe, you will see the glory of God?'" (John 11:40). One day, either in this lifetime[22] or in our life to come,[23] God's glory will pierce our

---

[20] John Piper, https:www.desiringgod.org/articles/god-is-always-doing-1000-things-in-your-life (accessed February 8, 2022).

[21] We saw this same principle in chapter 1, where Jesus delayed His arrival to Bethany to secure His own death on the cross. Jesus did not explain to the sisters why He waited because it would have been a burden too heavy for them to bear.

[22] The story of Joseph is an example of understanding God's mysterious ways in this life (Genesis 37-50). Thrown in a pit, sold into slavery, accused of attempted rape, left in prison—at the end of the story, Joseph realizes that all of it was necessary for God to preserve His covenant people (Genesis 50:20).

[23] Though the story of Joseph is an example of seeing God's mysterious ways unfold in a manner that makes sense, most of God's ways will confound us in this life. Like a great novel, we must wait until the end of the story to understand the details of each chapter along the way (Revelation 6:10-11).

clouded confusion. And His ways will shine brighter than we could have ever imagined. As William Cowper penned, "Judge not the Lord by feeble sense, but trust Him for His grace; Behind a frowning providence He hides a smiling face."

Sixth, confusion is necessary because it is the seedbed for greater faithfulness. Uncertainty births faith. Bewilderment forces us to trust someone greater than ourselves. Perplexity causes us to think outside the box of our strength and control. Mystery humbles us before our God. Where there is no wonder, no questions, no chaos—no confusion—there is no faith.

THE REAL-WORLD QUESTION

This leads to the real-world theological questions we must answer: How does faith respond when we are baffled by God's ways and puzzled by His designs? What does faith look like in the midst of perplexity? How does faith respond after we ask God, *why?* and wonder, *how long?*

Those are the questions we will answer in the next chapter.

5
THE ALL-WISE GOD WHO CONFOUNDS
HIS FOLLOWERS (PT. 2)

So when Jesus came, He found that he had already been in the tomb four days. Now Bethany was near Jerusalem, about two miles off; and many of the Jews had come to Martha and Mary, to console them concerning their brother. Martha therefore, when she heard that Jesus was coming, went to meet Him, but Mary stayed at the house. Martha then said to Jesus, "Lord, if You had been here, my brother would not have died. Even now I know that whatever You ask of God, God will give You." (John 11:17-22)

We ended the last chapter wrestling with the fact that God's sovereign decisions may, and often do, leave us perplexed. Every day we are reminded that God's judgments are unsearchable, His ways unfathomable, His mind unplumbable. Real-world theology knows that the sovereignty that brings so much comfort is the same sovereignty that confounds so often. And yet, it is in the caves of confusion where spiritual change is forged.

Where there is no confusion, there is no faith.

Real-world theology answers the questions: *What does faithfulness look like on the foggy days of life? How does faith respond when perplexed and wondering, confused and questioning?*

HOW DOES FAITH RESPOND WHEN GOD CONFOUNDS?

Martha's response to Jesus grants us insight into the answer. "Martha...said...'Even now I know that whatever You ask of God, God will give You'" (John 11:22).

On the surface, it might seem that Martha was asking, and maybe even expecting, Jesus to resurrect her brother. But that was not Martha's intent. We know that because of how Martha responded when Jesus commanded her to remove the stone from Lazarus' tomb. "Martha...said to Him, 'Lord, by this time there will be a stench, for he has been dead four days'" (John 11:39). Martha was not expecting Jesus to perform a resurrection miracle. She thought Lazarus would resurrect "on the last day" (John 11:24), but not this day.

Martha's statement, "Even now, I know that whatever You ask of God, God will give You," were words of faithful submission—how faith responds—when the clouds of confusion darken a believer's world.

FAITH FINDS CONFIDENCE IN CHRIST'S PERFECT INTERCESSION

First, when confused, faith finds confidence in Christ's perfect intercession. "Whatever You ask, God will give" (John 11:22).

Though confounded by Jesus' ways, Martha clung to the intimacy Christ shares with His Father and the interceding care He has for His people—trusting that the Father always grants His Son's requests. Whatever Jesus decided to ask on Martha's behalf, she was sure He would receive it. And this was not just Martha's opinion. Jesus Himself claimed this same interceding success in v. 42 when He, with complete assurance, said, "I knew that **You always hear Me**" (John 11:42, emphasis mine)—"always hear Me" in the sense of always agreeing with My prayers, always granting My petitions.

This is astounding! The Father heeds every prayer Jesus ever offers. Astounding, because no one else can claim such a thing for himself.

With everyone else, there is always the potential that sin will hinder their prayers (Psalm 66:18; Isaiah 59:2; James 4:3). But with Jesus, unanswered prayer is never a possibility. Every request Jesus makes always comes to fruition. Never is there a sin barrier that exists between Him and His Father. And thus, never will the Father turn a deaf ear to His Son. Jesus' sinless perfection secures every request He brings before His Father's throne on our behalf.

When tempted to wonder why the Lord seems far off, remember that Christ is interceding for you. You have not been forsaken. The Lord has not hidden Himself from you. Far from it! In Christ, you are standing before the Father's throne, represented by the sinless Son "who always lives to make intercession for [you]" (Hebrews 7:25). When you are confused, remember Christ is presenting your name and your need before His Father. Though mystified, remember His praying mercies. "We cannot afford to be ignorant of his intercession and the value of it for our souls, especially at those times when we feel perplexed by the trials and tribulations of this present evil age. As Scottish Presbyterian Robert Murray M'Cheyne (18:13-43) once famously said, 'If I could hear Christ praying for me in the next room, I would not fear a million enemies. Yet the distance makes no difference; he is praying for me.'"[24]

FAITH FINDS ASSURANCE IN CHRIST'S INFINITE WISDOM

Second, when confused, faith finds comfort in Christ's infinite wisdom—knowing that Christ only asks His Father for what is best.

"Martha said to Him, '**Whatever** You ask'" (John 11:22, emphasis mine). Martha was not telling Jesus how He should pray, or offering Him her opinions. She recognized her limitations and left the

---

[24] Mark Jones, *Knowing Christ* (Edinburg: Banner of Truth Trust, 2015), 179.

intercession to Jesus. *You know what we need most, Jesus. And I trust that whatever You ask from Your Father will be for our greatest good.*

When puzzled by God's ways, faith finds comfort in Christ's infinite wisdom. He knows His Father's perfect will for His children. And Christ will never ask for more than what His Father has promised to deliver.

FAITH FINDS CERTAINTY IN GOD'S SOVEREIGN POWER

Third, in the mire of confusion, faith finds certainty in God's sovereign power—assured that **everything**, even that which unsettles our soul, never occurs outside God's sovereign design. Martha's "whatever" is in the plural. *However big your request might be, Jesus; whatever details may be involved, whatever it will take to accomplish what You ask; I am trusting that whatever you bring before Your Father's throne on my behalf, "God will give You"* (John 11:22). Martha rested on the Father's omnipotence, sovereignty, and wisdom.

For three days, Martha wondered like Job, "Why do You hide Your face and consider me Your enemy?" (Job 13:24). For three days, she asked with the Psalmist, "How long, O LORD? Will You forget me forever?" (Psalm 13:1). For three days, she stared at her brother's tomb in tears and disbelief. For three days, she wondered why Jesus' promise failed.

But now, Martha confessed her sovereign Lord's control. Whatever Jesus asked His Father to do, it would be done—and it would be good.

CALM AND CONFUSED

Confusion is unnerving. Chaos, upsetting and uncomfortable. Yet, the Christian need not fear. There is a spiritual calmness available for God's children. Peace, not based upon the certainty of the moment, but based upon the steadfastness of our Lord.

Though sorrowful, Martha did not lash out in anger when Jesus arrived. Though puzzled, she did not berate Him or question His delay. She accused Jesus of no wrong. She spoke with no bitterness and harbored no resentment. Rather, in faith, Martha chose calmness during chaos—**and so can we.**

Confused, yet calm—because our Savior never ceases to intercede on our behalf. Confused, yet calm—because in the Lord's infinite wisdom, He allows only that which will shine His glory most brightly. Confused, yet calm—because nothing happens outside God's sovereign reign. Confused, yet calm—because "to Him be the glory forever. Amen" (Romans 11:36).

6
THE LOVING GOD WHO TREMBLES IN HIS SOUL

When Jesus therefore saw her weeping, and the Jews who came with her also weeping, He was deeply moved in spirit and was troubled, and said, "Where have you laid him?" They said to Him, "Lord, come and see." Jesus wept. So the Jews were saying, "See how He loved him!" But some of them said, "Could not this man, who opened the eyes of the blind man, have kept this man also from dying?" So Jesus, again being deeply moved within, came to the tomb. Now it was a cave, and a stone was lying against it. (John 11:33-38)

We do not fully realize Christ's love for us. How could we?

A divine love that sacrificed a face-to-face relationship with the Father (John 1:1)—who can comprehend? A heavenly love that incarnated itself in the frailty of created man (2 Corinthians 8:9)—who can grasp? An eternal love that chose death, and suffering, and wrath for the sake of sinners—who can fathom?

Christ's love is too wonderful to fully appreciate, too vast to wrap our minds around. Its heights reach to the heavens, and its depths tunnel into the unknown (Ephesians 3:18). And though real-world theology will never fully plumb the love Christ has for us, we still must try—and treasure what we find.

A LOVING SAVIOR AND HIS TROUBLED SOUL

As John 11:33 opens, Jesus has finally arrived in Bethany, ending the four days of silence, questions, and confusion Mary and Martha experienced since their brother Lazarus died. If you already know the story, you know what Jesus is about to do: He will wield His power over the grave, reach into Sheol and snatch a friend from death's grip. The Lord of life is about to conquer the king of terrors. The Master of the grave will soon empty Lazarus' tomb.

This is why Jesus' emotional response in verse 33 comes out of nowhere. John tells us that Jesus "was troubled" *(tarasso)*[25] as He eyed Lazarus' tomb. Jesus was shaken. Disturbed. Repulsed by what He saw. A heaviness engulfed His soul. One translator put it this way, "Jesus gave way to such distress of spirit as made his body tremble."[26] The always calm Jesus became agitated, even horrified. He trembled. He shook.

Compare this reaction to what Jesus commanded His Apostles in John 14:1, "Do not let your heart be **troubled** *[tarasso]*" (John 14:1, emphasis mine). But now, as Jesus stood in front of Lazarus' grave, what Jesus commanded His Apostles not to be, **He is.** The one who once slept soundly while a storm raged around Him, now churned on the inside. The one who stood boldly before the demonic realm, was now distressed, unnerved, distraught—a spiritual agitation that showed itself with tears running down Jesus' face in verse 35, "Jesus wept."[27]

---

[25] A living picture of this word is found in John 5:7, where a tranquil pool is "stirred up" and agitated.

[26] As quoted in R. Kent Hughes, *John: That You May Believe* (Wheaton: Crossway Books, 1999), 285.

[27] John used a different word for Jesus' weeping in verse 35 than he did for the weeping crowd in v. 33. Jesus' tears were not the loud, public tears of verse 33. Jesus' tears were the quiet and personal tears of a sobbing Savior. Why the difference in wording? Because John knows Jesus wept for a different reason than the crowd. They cried because Lazarus died. Jesus wept because Lazarus would soon live.

We must ask, *why?* Why did Jesus weep? Why did God's Son experience such inner turmoil? We must ask, *what?* What shocked incarnate God to the point of tears? What disturbed His tranquil soul? We know what it wasn't. It wasn't Lazarus' death—because Jesus knew He would rectify that in a matter of minutes. It wasn't Mary and Martha's sorrow—because Jesus knew He would soon give them their brother back.

Then what was it?

OUR SAVIOR WEEPS BECAUSE OF HIS COMING CROSS

The crowd thought Jesus wept because He arrived too late to save a friend. They thought He mourned because He was not going to see Lazarus again. Therefore "some of them said, 'Could not [Jesus]…have kept this man from also dying?'" (John 11:38).

But the reality was this: Jesus was not weeping because He would never see Lazarus again. No, He shed tears, on this day, because He **would see** Lazarus again. Jesus wept, not because Lazarus died, but because Lazarus was about to live.

Jesus wept because He knew what He must do if He was going to call Lazarus from the grave: for Lazarus to rise, Jesus must die. He must pay the required cost to fix sin's rupture, and break death's chains, and satisfy God's wrath.[28] Jesus knew, once He called Lazarus from his grave, there could be no turning back. The cross was His necessary fate.

As Jesus stood before Lazarus' tomb, He trembled because He peered into **His own demise**. This is why John describes Lazarus'

---

[28] Luke 19:41 is the only other passage in the Gospels where we read that Jesus cried. There, Jesus wept because God would judge Jerusalem using the armies of Rome. Here in John 11, Jesus wept because of a far severer judgment that was about to fall—judgment from the hand of His Father that would be meted out upon Christ, in full, for the sin of others (Isaiah 53:10).

and Jesus' tombs with eerie similarities. Both men will be confined to a cave. Both will have a stone door lock their dead corpses inside (compare John 11:38 with 20:1). Both will have their bodies bound with wrappings and faces covered with a cloth (compare John 11:44 with 19:40 and 20:6).

Why the similarities? Because Lazarus' tomb was a foreshadowing of Jesus' own fate—and it startled Jesus like never before. As Mark Jones wrote, "Jesus knew that if Lazarus were to come out of the grave, then He Himself must enter it. No wonder 'Jesus wept.'"[29]

And we know it was the cross that caused Jesus' soul to tremble, because each time John uses "troubled" (*tarasso*) to describe Jesus, it is always with reference to His coming death.

"My soul has become **troubled** [*tarasso*]; and what shall I say, 'Father, save Me from this hour'? But for this purpose I came to this hour." (John 12:27, emphasis mine)

"I know the ones I have chosen; but it is that the Scripture may be fulfilled, 'HE WHO EATS MY BREAD HAS LIFTED UP HIS HEEL AGAINST ME'...When Jesus had said this, He became **troubled** [*tarasso*] in spirit." (John 13:18, 21, emphasis mine)

Christ's commitment to the cross caused His tears to flow on this day.[30] His saving love for the sinner shook His soul. He knew His Father would soon forsake Him (Psalm 22:1). He knew the crushing hand of God would soon fall upon Him (Isaiah 53:10). Isaiah was right; only through "the anguish of [the Servant's] soul...[would] He justify the many" (Isaiah 53:11). And for Jesus, that anguish of

---

[29] Jones, *Knowing*, 141.
[30] John is the only Gospel not to record Jesus' tearful prayers in the Garden of Gethsemane (Matthew 26:36-46; Mark 14:32-42; Luke 22:39-46). One reason is because John didn't have to. Rather than recording one night of agony, John showed that Jesus' Gethsemane struggle "was the culmination of a struggle that preceded it." Merrill C. Tenney, "John and Acts" in *The Expositors Bible Commentary* (Grand Rapids: Zondervan, 1981), 129.

love began in Bethany, as He stood before Lazarus' grave, with tears streaming down His face.

Let us never take our Savior's love for granted. Let us never think He "approached [His sacrifice for us] in a spirit of untroubled calm."[31] Christ's love is no sappy Hallmark greeting, or a domesticated man-centered infatuation. His is a dying love, wrath-bearing love, atoning love, substitutionary love, death-defeating love, resurrection-securing love—and thus, a soul-trembling love.

COMPREHENDING THE INCOMPREHENSIBLE

Do you see why we will never be able to fully grasp Christ's love? His love for us cost Him everything! Words on a page cannot do this justice. Our puny minds cannot fathom all the implications. His love is boundless, bottomless, endless. As the hymnwriter penned,

> Could we with ink the ocean fill
>
> And were the skies of parchment made
>
> Were every stalk on earth a quill
>
> And every man a scribe by trade
>
> To write the love of God above
>
> Would drain the ocean dry
>
> Nor could the scroll contain the whole
>
> Though stretched from sky to sky.[32]

---

[31] Morris, *Reflections*, 416. Milne adds, "For in his death he must not only face the reality of human finitude, the ending of his mission, the mockery of his enemies in whose eyes he will die a failure, and in addition the appalling physical and mental suffering of death by crucifixion. Beyond all that he must also face the Father himself, the one to whom he has been inseparably bound for all eternity, not in the warm embrace of his everlasting love, but in the terror of his holy and righteous wrath. He must in fact become the object of divine rejection, the bearer of the implacable antipathy to sin and evil of the ever-living God. He was troubled. Indeed, he had reason to be." Bruce Milne, *The Message of John* (Downers Grove: InterVarsity Press, 2020), 189.

[32] Frederick Martin Lehman, *Love of God is Greater Far.*

To fully comprehend the incomprehensible is an impossible task. And yet we must still try. Because when we do, our hearts will burst forth in worship (Psalm 63:9), our doubts will be relieved (Romans 5:10), our fears removed (Romans 8:35-39), our soul satisfied (Psalm 63:10), and our lives changed (2 Corinthians 5:14-15)—for there is no greater motivation to live for our Lord than to be overwhelmed by His soul-trembling love for us.

7

THE GRACIOUS GOD WHO PROMISES
FUTURE HOPE

Jesus said to her, "Your brother will rise again." Martha said to Him, "I know that he will rise again in the resurrection on the last day." Jesus said to her, "I am the resurrection and the life; he who believes in Me will live even if he dies, and everyone who lives and believes in Me will never die. Do you believe this?" She said to Him, "Yes, Lord; I have believed that You are the Christ, the Son of God, even He who comes into the world"....Jesus said, "Remove the stone." Martha, the sister of the deceased, said to Him, "Lord, by this time there will be a stench, for he has been dead four days. Jesus said to her, "Did I not say to you that if you believe, you will see the glory of God?" So they removed the stone. Then Jesus raised His eyes, and said, "Father, I thank You that You have heard Me. I knew that You always hear Me; but because of the people standing around I said it, so that they may believe that You sent Me." When He had said these things, He cried out with a loud voice, "Lazarus, come forth." The man who had died came forth, bound hand and foot with wrappings, and his face was wrapped around with a cloth. Jesus said to them, "Unbind him, and let him go." (John 11:23-27, 40-44)

Hope. It's a powerful motivator. It's what replaces worry with calmness (Romans 15:13), despair with joy (Psalm 42:5), and cowardice with courage (Romans 12:12). Our God is "the God of hope" (Romans 15:13). The Gospel is "the hope of glory" (Colossians 1:27). Faith is "a living hope" (1 Peter 1:3) that promises to never disappoint (Romans 5:5). Out of everyone in our world, Christians should be the most hopeful—confident that our future is secured by a good and sovereign Savior.

HAVE WE LOST OUR HOPE?

And yet, as a pastor, I often see disappointment written on so many Christian faces. Hope seems to be an elusive ring dangling outside our outstretched hand. Believers disheartened by government leaders. Christian parents fearful of the world their children will grow up in. Church families ruptured over pettiness and infighting. Conversations filled more with complaining than with Christ.

And the effect? Christian joy has been dampened; Gospel energy, smothered; spiritual unity, fractured; the light of Christ, overshadowed by the gloom of our world. *Why* is the question. Why has despair filled so many Christian hearts? Why has dejection squelched so much Gospel work? Why has division taken root in so many Christian churches?

One reason is that our hope has been exposed—and it has been found wanting. We have tied too much happiness to the promises of this world. We have lived by sight, rather than faith, for far too long. We have allowed our affections for the temporal to root too deep and have become satisfied by earthly pleasures too much.

We have forgotten that our "hope is laid up...in heaven" (Colossians 1:5). We've failed to "fix our hope completely on the grace to be brought to us at the revelation of Jesus Christ" (1 Peter 1:13). We've unmoored our joy from our coming resurrection and Christ's promised return (and all the blessings that entails), and have instead anchored our hope in the here and now.

It's no wonder despair is written on so many Christian faces. We've been hoping in the wrong things.

CHRISTIAN HOPE IS GROUNDED IN FUTURE GLORY

For most of John 11, there has been no hope. For four days, private tears streamed down Mary and Martha's cheeks, while the crowd's public sobs rang throughout the town (John 11:33). The sisters have been confused: *Why would Jesus let our brother, His friend, die? Why would Jesus not come immediately to save us from our grief?* You can hear the pain in the sisters' hearts, as they both told Jesus, "Lord, if You had been here, my brother would not have died" (John 11:21, 32). Is there anything more hopeless than death? More painful than loss? More final than a sealed grave?

And yet, what was Jesus' answer to the sisters' sorrow? "Your brother will rise again" (John 11:23). He gives them hope—hope that looks to the future. Christian hope is always grounded in future glory.

Think of Israel. As destruction marched toward the Promised Land, what hope did the Lord hold out for them? "Your dead will live; their corpses will rise. You who lie in the dust, awake and shout for joy" (Isaiah 26:19). During political upheaval, the Lord promised His people a future resurrection.

Take Job. On what did he rest his hope amid failing health? "Even after my skin is destroyed, yet from my flesh I shall see God" (Job 19:26).

And then there is Paul. Why did he not lose heart in the ministry? Because he looked to "an eternal weight of glory far beyond all comparison" (2 Corinthians 4:18).

Gospel hope is always forward-looking. It's eschatological. It's future.[33]

This is why Jesus gave His grand promise in verses 25 and 26. At the moment of Mary and Martha's deepest grief, Jesus offered them His greatest promise, "I am the resurrection and the life; he who

---

[33] To put this principle in John Calvin's words, "no man has made much progress in the school of Christ who does not look forward with joy to the day of death and final resurrection." John Calvin, *Institutes of the Christian Religion* (Westminster Press, 1970), 3.9.5.

believes in Me will live even if he dies, and everyone who lives and believes in Me will never die" (John 11:25-26).

Life in this fallen world has only one ending: physical death—health stricken, lives lost, freedoms removed, dreams dashed, plans changed. What is Christ's answer? Anchor your hope in your future glory.

FUTURE GLORY IS NOT WISHFUL THINKING

"I am the resurrection and the life" is a claim to deity (Deuteronomy 32:39; 1 Samuel 2:6; Psalm 49:15)—Jesus claiming to be the source of our future resurrection and the fountainhead of our eternal life. A staggering statement, eclipsed only by the stunning nature of the miracle that followed.

Each detail of Lazarus' resurrection is meaningful. Each instills hope for the believer.

First, John noted Lazarus' decay and stench, since Lazarus had been dead four days (John 11:39). Astounding. The Christian need not fear; no amount of decay will hinder Christ's resurrection power.

Second, Jesus indicated Lazarus' resurrection was His Father's will (John 11:41-42). Comforting. Our future resurrection will not only be the work of Christ, but also the will of the Father.

Third, Jesus "**cried out** with a loud voice" (John 11:43, emphasis mine). Jesus had Isaiah's warning in mind, that "mediums and the spiritists...whisper and mutter" their incantations (Isaiah 8:19). Jesus is no spiritist—He's the Lord of life. But even more than that, Christ's shout was a foreshadowing of what He will one day do for every believer—a preview of His "cry of command" (1 Thessalonians 4:16) that will be heard throughout the entire earth when He returns. Assuring. Christ possesses supreme power over death and will one day issue a resurrection command that will reach every grave throughout this world (John 5:28-29).

Fourth, Jesus called Lazarus by name, "**Lazarus**, come forth" (John 11:43, emphasis mine). Jesus could have simply said "come forth," but He didn't. He individualized His call. Humbling. Christ's resurrection power will be personal. As Jesus promised, "Everyone who beholds the Son and believes in Him will have eternal life, and I myself will raise him up on the last day…I will raise him up on the last day" (John 6:40, 44). Christ will leave no believer in the ground. He will forget none of His own on that final day.

Our future glory is not wishful thinking. It is a settled fact—powerfully confirmed when the Lord of life shattered Sheol's chains. Jesus' promise is true, "he who believes in Me will live even if he dies" (John 11:25).

WHERE IS YOUR HOPE?

Yes, this world is spiraling further and further into sin. And yes, disappointments abound—they always have and always will. And there are, no doubt, great sorrows and deep heartaches in our future. But rather than stealing our Christian hope, and smothering our Gospel energy, and sullying our Christian testimony, each sorrow should strengthen our expectation for that glorious day when our Lord "will swallow up death for all time, and the Lord GOD will wipe tears away from all faces…And it will be said in that day, 'Behold, this is our God for whom we have waited that He might save us. This is the LORD for whom we have waited; Let us rejoice and be glad in His salvation'" (Isaiah 25:7, 9).

Real-world theology waits for that coming day with expectancy and confidence, refusing to become downcast with despair. It turns our eyes to Christ's eternal salvation, away from the sorrows of the moment. It anchors our hope on the firm promises of glory, not the shifting sands of this fallen world.

Oh Christian, be hopeful—no, be the most hopeful person in this world—because our hope is not in the present, but in a Person, a Savior, a Sovereign, who has promised a future glory and an everlasting kingdom to all who have come to Him in saving faith. Heed Peter's command and "fix your hope completely on the grace to be brought to you at the revelation of Jesus Christ" (1 Peter 1:13). Believe Jesus' promise, "I am the resurrection and the life" (John 11:25).

8

THE SAVING GOD
WHOM SINNERS REJECT

Therefore many of the Jews who came to Mary, and saw what He had done, believed in Him. But some of them went to the Pharisees and told them the things which Jesus had done. (John 11:45-46)

Why do people reject the Gospel of Jesus? Or to make the question more personal: *Why do my family members, who live under the guilt of their sin, refuse full forgiveness and complete pardon? Why are my closest friends apathetic to being reconciled to their Creator—the one who made them, and owns them, and loves them? Why do my neighbors, who search endlessly for satisfaction in this life, reject fullness of life in Christ?*

These are perplexing questions because, to us who believe the Gospel, rejecting Jesus makes no sense. Christ's Gospel is not just good news, it's the greatest news—that Creator God, though holy and transcendent, sent His eternal Son in grace and love; and this Son, Jesus, willingly and lovingly lived the sinless life we could never live (Hebrews 4:15), paid the penalty for sin we could never pay (Isaiah 53:10), defeated an enemy we could never defeat (1 Corinthians 15:55, 57), to secure an eternal destiny we could never earn (Romans 6:23).

Why would anyone reject that message? It's glorious! It's filled with grace and mercy and hope. It's grounded on supernatural love, promising what no other gospel can promise.

Yet, we've all heard those words: *Your gospel is not for me. It's not what I'm looking for. It's not what I want or need.*

And so we leave those conversations wondering, *Did I say something wrong?* We ask ourselves, *Was there some deficiency in me? Was I not convincing enough? Or passionate enough? Or logical enough? Was it because I couldn't answer all the questions posed? Was it because I said something offensive? Maybe I moved too quickly to talk about sin? Or perhaps I didn't focus enough on God's love?*

Why do people reject the Gospel? is the question. *What are we to do about it?* is the application.

THE CLIMACTIC MIRACLE

As John 11:45 opens, Jesus has just performed the most spectacular miracle of His ministry, the climactic sign of John's presentation of Jesus as God's Son. With just three words Sheol was shattered, and a brother, still wrapped in his death garments, stood alive and upright outside the tomb he had been confined to for the past four days.

No one—not even Mary and Martha—expected Lazarus to walk out of that cave (John 11:39). This was why the crowd of mourners stood in stunned silence, paralyzed by what they had just witnessed. Shocked because the King of Life now stood in their midst. Dumbstruck, trying to make sense of what just happened. A living, breathing, walking Lazarus was "Exhibit A" that Jesus was no mere man. He was who He claimed to be: the long awaited Messiah; the Son of God, sent from heaven to save the world from sin and death (John 3:16; 5:25, 28-29).

This is what miracles were meant to do: confirm the words and claims of the miracle-worker (Exodus 4:4-5; 1 Kings 17:23-24). Miracles were God's credentials that His messenger could be trusted.[34] It was no different with Jesus.

---

[34] "The biblical 'miracles of power' do not occur haphazardly, for no rhyme or reason, in salvation history. To the contrary, the Bible suggests that they serve the revelatory process of authenticating the credentials of the human organs of special revelation who

"The works which the Father has given Me to accomplish—the very works that I do—testify about Me, that the Father has sent Me." (John 5:46)

"The works that I do in My Father's name, these testify of Me." (John 10:25, 37-38)

Given Jesus' miracles, how could any doubt His claims?

WE EXPECT FAITH, DON'T WE?

We expect this miraculous story to conclude in saving faith, don't we? How else could a story like this end? How else could the crowd respond to a dead man walking? Which is why verse 45 comes as no surprise, "Many of the Jews who came to Mary, and saw what He had done, believed in Him" (John 11:45). Some Jews, once opposed to Jesus, now accept Him, believe Him, and love Him. This is the expected ending.

But this is not where John ends this story. The shocking ending is that some grew angry toward Jesus, irate that He had just given a brother back to a grieving family. This is the group that immediately "went to the Pharisees and told them the things which Jesus had done" (John 11:46). This was no evangelistic testimony. They brought a hostile report to the most aggressive haters of Jesus—the Pharisees—the very ones who had "sent officers to seize Him" the last time Jesus was in Jerusalem (John 7:32).

Their plan was simple: throw fuel on the Pharisees' fiery hatred for Jesus. A plan that worked to perfection. "Therefore the chief priests and the Pharisees convened a council, and were saying, 'What are we doing? For this man is performing many signs'...So from that day on they planned together to kill him" (John 11:47, 53). The one who conquered death had now been sentenced to die.

---

brought men the redemptive truth of God." Robert Reymond, *A New Systematic Theology of the Christian Faith* (Thomas Nelson Publishers: Nashville, 1998), 409.

The same Jesus. The same Lazarus. The same tomb. The same miracle. The same witnesses. And yet two entirely different responses.

The crowd's rejection may even be more stunning than the miracle itself.

HARD HEARTS AND BLIND EYES

Why do people reject the Gospel? Because their hearts are hard to its message, their eyes are spiritually blind to its Savior, and their wills are unmoved by its appeal.

If there is anything John 11 teaches us, it is this: "When people do not want to believe they will always find a way of discounting even the strongest evidence…The reaction of unbelief is always to ignore the power of God, even if it is at work before one's very eyes."[35] In this case, even a dead man walking could not convince sinners of their need of a Savior (Luke 16:31).[36]

SOMETHING GREATER THAN SHEOL-SHATTERING POWER

So where does that leave us and our witnessing efforts? If raising someone from the dead did not change a sinner's heart, what hope for success do we have in our Gospel witness?

Real-world theology understands that every evangelistic success resides in the omnipotent God, who uses the proclamation of His Gospel, to transform an unbelieving heart.

We do not have the authority to call dead bodies from a grave like Jesus did. But that's okay, because faith comes by hearing, not seeing (Romans 10:17). We have something more significant than Sheol-shattering power. We have Christ's Gospel and Christ's

---

[35] Morris, *Reflections*, 420.

[36] "The sight of a person clothed with the splendor of heaven or the terrors of hell would surprise and alarm, but it would never convert a soul." Charles Simeon, "Matthew" in *Horae Homileticae* (London: Holdsworth and Ball, 1855), 12:566.

Spirit—which together do what not even the most stunning miracle could do: expose a sinners' spiritual need (John 6:35), open deaf ears to hear the Savior's call (John 6:44), and replace a dead heart of sin with a living heart filled with repentance and faith (John 6:63).

NOT WEAK OR MEAGER, BUT DIVINELY POWERFUL

We must think highly of the Gospel. It is not weak or meager, but divinely powerful. It is "the power of God for salvation" (Romans 1:16), the means the Spirit uses to save a sinner's soul.

Remember, our Lord does not hold us responsible to change an unbelieving heart. He has not called us to answer every question a skeptic might pose. He has not commissioned us to argue someone into the kingdom with clever words or foolproof logic.

Our calling is much simpler than that: speak our Savior's Gospel faithfully and wait upon the Spirit to perform a resurrection even greater than Lazarus'—a resurrection of the spiritually dead to newness of life.

9

THE SOVEREIGN GOD WHO RULES ALL EVIL

Therefore the chief priests and the Pharisees convened a council, and were saying, "What are we doing? For this man is performing many signs. If we let Him go on like this, all men will believe in Him, and the Romans will come and take away both our place and our nation." But one of them, Caiaphas, who was high priest that year, said to them, "You know nothing at all, nor do you take into account that it is expedient for you that one man die for the people, and that the whole nation not perish." Now he did not say this on his own initiative, but being high priest that year, he prophesied that Jesus was going to die for the nation, and not for the nation only, but in order that He might also gather together into one the children of God who are scattered abroad. So from that day on they planned together to kill Him. (John 11:47-53)

"This is my Father's world: O let me ne'er forget. That though the wrong seems oft so strong, God is the ruler yet."

This stanza from Maltbie Babcock's hymn, *This is My Father's World*, has comforted many Christians since it was published in 1915. It has served as a needed reminder that though sin is real, it is ruled—ruled by a sovereign God who only allows evil to exist when it brings good to His people and glory to His name (Romans 8:28).

But is this stanza true? After all, horrible atrocities litter our world's history. The carnage of interpersonal sin is strewn from city to city, and house to house. Injustices define many nations. Wickedness headlines every news outlet. Sin hurts. It tears families apart, brings heartache and pain, and wreaks havoc and chaos. As Babcock writes, sin is "oft so strong." We know that part of the hymn is accurate because we've all experienced it firsthand. But is the next phrase true as well? "God is the ruler yet."

The answer is, *yes*—and the way John concludes chapter 11 proves this point.

A CONVENED COUNCIL, NOT A CELEBRATORY SUPPER

As verse 47 opens, Lazarus' resurrection story does not end like we might expect it to: around a table, with friends and family eating a celebratory meal, rejoicing because a brother lives. This ending is much different: in the Hall of Hewn Stone, where the supreme court of Israel has gathered to finalize the most heinous act ever to be committed in all of world history—the execution of God's perfect Son.

Nothing is more wicked: to condemn to death the Lord of Life; to scourge, beat, and humiliate the one who had just shown a family divine mercy and grace; to call for Christ's crucifixion, and then watch Him hang with a haughty smugness—this is "the most spectacular sin....the apex of evil."[37] And yet, **this** is the conclusion to the joyous story of Lazarus' resurrection.

JEALOUSY, NOT JOY

Note the "therefore" that connects Lazarus' resurrection in verses 43-44 to the animosity and evil that fills verses 47-53. "**Therefore** the chief priests and the Pharisees convened a council" (John 11:47, emphasis mine).

---

[37] John Piper, *Spectacular Sins: And Their Global Purpose in the Glory of Christ* (Crossway Books: Wheaton, 2008), 12.

The Sanhedrin convened an emergency meeting **because** Jesus had called Lazarus from the grave; **because** He gave Mary and Martha their brother back; **because** Jesus had performed the climactic miracle of His ministry—sealing every sign He had offered Israel, proving beyond all doubt His identity as Messiah, the Son of God whom He claimed to be.[38]

Joy should have filled the chief priests' hearts—their Messiah had arrived! And yet, they were jealous, not joyous; afraid they would soon lose their standing among the people and place of prominence within the nation.

This is why they asked each other, "What are we doing?" (John 11:47). *Why are we letting this man live? Why are we holding back our punches?* "For this man is performing many signs" (John 11:47). Though Jesus' miracles infuriated them, the Sanhedrin could not question their legitimacy. How could they? Jesus' power had gone public. The lame walked. The blind saw. And now the dead lived.

They knew the inevitable outcome if Jesus continued unhindered. "If we let Him go on like this, all men will believe in Him" (11:48). Jesus' popularity would grow, and their influence would wane. And even worse, "the Romans will come and take away both our place and our nation" (11:48).[39]

AN EVIL PRIEST, APPOINTED BY A SOVEREIGN GOD

Something must be done. Even more, *someone needs to die.* That was the conclusion reached by Caiaphas—the man who had been illegitimately appointed high priest by the Roman Prefect Valerius Gratus. This was how deep the Sanhedrin's depravity ran. The high priest, meant to mediate man-to-God, had been installed as a political puppet whose strings were pulled by Caesar's hand.

---

[38] See chapter 6, which explains the purpose of Jesus' miracles.
[39] "Their concern is a legitimate one validated by history…the Romans ultimately did take away their temple and nation, in A.D. 70." Craig S. Keener, *The Bible Background Commentary* (InterVarsity Press: Downers Grove, 1993).

And yet, what does Scripture assure us about every ruler—even evil rulers?

> "It is [the God of heaven] who changes the times and the epochs; He removes kings and establishes kings." (Daniel 2:21)

> "The Most High is ruler over the realm of mankind, and bestows it on whom He wishes." (Daniel 4:17)

> "For there is no authority except from God, and those which exist are established by God." (Romans 13:1)

From a human perspective, Gratus had appointed this evil priest to his post. And yet, behind that prefect's choice was the decree of a sovereign God.[40] Why? Because Caiaphas would be the one to suggest the unthinkable and monstrous: the execution of God's Son. In Caiaphas' words, "It is expedient…that one man die for the people, and that the whole nation not perish" (John 11:50).

WHEN GOOD IS EVIL AND EVIL IS GOOD

Does this not sound like the politics of our day? Where leaders no longer fear God; where pragmatic results have replaced conviction of sin; where justice is deemed relative, and morals plied to fit one's own ideology; where one is willing to break the law for the sake of political maneuvering; where evil is deemed good and good is called evil (Isaiah 5:20).

And yet whatever evil we may be experiencing today, however corrupt we might think our world has become, it is nothing compared to the evil Caiaphas proposed. *Death to Jesus* was his motto. *Murder the Messiah* was his slogan.

The evil was dark within the Hall of Hewn Stone. Hardened hearts had convened. Jealous spirits had spoken. Seared consciences had

---

[40] John included the phrase "that year" to emphasize God's sovereign control of the situation, much the same way he used the phrases "that day" (John 11:53) and "that hour" (John 14:20; 16:23, 26). Days, hours, and years belong to the Lord.

calculated. And a foolish scheme[41] had been offered by a wicked high priest. There was only one verdict for this court—**Jesus must die.**

"GOD IS THE RULER YET"

But remember Babcock's phrase, "God is the ruler yet." This is why John adds his editorial note, "now [Caiaphas] did not say this on his own initiative" (John 11:51). Despite Caiaphas' evil, God was at work, divinely intervening, using the high priest's sin-laden heart for His own saving design. There was a reason God allowed Caiaphas' scandalous plan to hatch—so that Christ would fulfill the very purpose of His coming and accomplish the greatest good for His people: His sacrificial death for sin.

As John Piper put it, "People lift their hand to rebel against the Most High only to find that their rebellion is unwitting service in the wonderful designs of God...The hardened disobedience of men's hearts leads not to the frustration of God's plans, but to their fruition."[42]

AN EVIL PRIEST SPEAKS GOSPEL TRUTH

John called Caiaphas' evil plan a "prophecy" in verse 51. Not that John considered Caiaphas a true or righteous prophet. No, Caiaphas was a Balaam-like prophet—one who, while trying to speak evil against God's people, could only pronounce blessing upon them (Numbers 22). Caiaphas was right—one man would indeed die for the people (John 11:50)—but not the way Caiaphas intended.

Caiaphas intended for Jesus' death to douse any anti-Roman revolt that was stirring because of Jesus' miraculous power. But God had

---

[41] Caiaphas' plan is an example of the foolishness of sin and blindness of the sinner. Jesus had just shown His power over the grave by raising Lazarus from the dead, and yet Caiaphas believed he had the power to kill the Lord of life (Romans 1:28).

[42] John Piper, *Desiring God* (Multnomah: Sisters, 1996), 37.

bigger plans. Yes, Jesus would die, but not to stay Rome's hand. Jesus would die to extinguish God's wrath. He would "die for the nation" (John 11:51), fulfilling that grand substitutionary promise in Isaiah 53 (Isaiah 53:5).

SIN ACCOMPLISHES GOD'S SOVEREIGN DECREE[43]

Caiaphas chose his evil, but God had already predestined its good. Using Caiaphas' hardened heart, the Lord set in motion the fulfillment of His Abrahamic Covenant (Genesis 12:3). Using Caiaphas' jealous spirit, the Lord would bring salvation to the shores of the Gentiles (Isaiah 2:2; 49:6; 56:7-8). Using Caiaphas' seared conscience, Christ would accomplish exactly what He promised in John 10, to "lay down His life for the sheep" and gather sinners into "one flock with one shepherd" (John 10:11, 16). Proverbs 16:4 is true, "The LORD has made everything for its own purpose, even the wicked for the day of evil."

And thus, the story ends where it must, with the religious leaders ratifying Caiaphas' wicked plan. "So from that day on they planned to kill Him" (John 11:53). The council, which was supposed to uphold the law, had sacrificed justice on the altar of political expediency and sentenced an innocent man to death because of selfish preservation.

Yet we know what was happening in heaven at this exact moment, don't we? God the Father was laughing in disgust at this proud court, scoffing at their foolish plans (Psalm 2:4)—because, unbeknownst to them, they were fulfilling what He had determined from eternity past. They were living out Proverbs 19:21, "Many plans are in man's heart, but the counsel of the LORD will stand."

---

[43] The Westminster Shorter Catechism describes God's sovereign decree in question #7:
  Question #7: What are the decrees of God?
  Answer: The decrees of God are his eternal purpose according to the counsel of his will, whereby, for his own glory, he hath foreordained whatsoever comes to pass.

The hymnwriter was right, "though the wrong seems oft so strong, God is the ruler yet."

THE UNDERSIDE OF A BEAUTIFUL TAPESTRY

Real-world theology sees sin as the necessary underside of the beautiful tapestry God is weaving throughout all human history. Like strings that have no rhyme or reason, thread that has no pattern or plan, when the expert weaver finally finishes His masterpiece and flips over His work—all the chaos makes sense. And it is perfect, breathtaking, and good.

The poem, *The Master Weaver*[44], says it well:

My life is but a weaving

Between my God and me

I cannot choose the colors He weaveth steadily

Oft' times He weaveth sorrow

And I in foolish pride

Forget He sees the upper

And I the underside.

Not 'til the loom is silent

And the shuttles cease to fly

Will God unroll the canvas

And reveal the reason why.

The dark threads are as needful

In the weaver's skillful hand

As the threads of gold and silver

---

[44]Author unknown, though often attributed to Corrie Ten Boom.

In the pattern He has planned

He knows, He loves, He cares

Nothing this truth can dim

He gives the very best to those

Who leave the choice to Him

Yes, sin is real, but it is ruled—ruled by our good and caring God, who is weaving every injustice, wicked scheme, and sinful hurt into His designed masterpiece for His people.

Oh Christian, take heart and "rest patiently in the Lord. [Because] the very things that at one time seem likely to hurt [us], shall prove in the end to be for [our] gain."[45]

------

[45] Ryle, "John," 293.

CONCLUSION
TRUE THEOLOGY IS REAL-WORLD THEOLOGY

I hope you have been able to see that true theology is not irrelevant, boring, or cold. It is personal—the story of God working in the lives of His people. It is vital—the only grid through which we can rightly evaluate the world. And it is breathtaking—revealing a God whose ways and purposes are far greater than our own.

True theology cannot be confined to the ivory towers of the academic elite. It is no scholarly exercise or theoretical musing. No, theology is for everyone—real people, asking real questions, experiencing real emotions, needing real answers—who see the glory of God in everyday life, even in the midst of chaos, confusion, and sorrow.

And so I end where I began, asking the question, *What kind of theologian are you?*

May your answer be, *I am the real-world theologian God has called me to be—one who thinks highly and often of my God; who considers my story as His story; and is humbled by His wisdom, broken by His love, faithful when confounded by His ways, bold because of His sovereignty, and fearless for His Gospel.*

BIBLIOGRAPHY

Barrett, C.K. *The Gospel According to St. John*. 2nd ed. Philadelphia: Westminster Press, 1978.

Beasley-Murray, George R. *John*. Vol. 36 of WBC. Waco: WordBooks, 1987.

Borchert, Gerald. *John 1-11*. The New American Commentary. Nashville: Broadman & Holman Publishers, 1996.

Brown, Jeannine K. *The Gospels as Stories*. Grand Rapids: Baker Academic, 2020.

Bruce, F.F. *The Gospel & Epistles of John*. Grand Rapids: Eerdman's Publishing, 1994.

Calvin, John. *Institutes of the Christian Religion*. Edited by John T. McNeil. Westminster Press, 1970.

Carson, D.A. *The Gospel According to John*. The Pillar New Testament Commentary. Grand Rapids: Eerdman's Publishing, 1991.

Carter, Matt Carter and Josh Wredberg. *Christ-Centered Exposition: Exalting Jesus in John*. Holman: Nashville, 2017.

Edwards, Jonathan. *The End for Which God Created the World: Updated to Modern English*. Edited by Jason Dollar. Westbow Press, 2018.

Foxe, John. *Foxe's Christian Martyrs of the World*. Chicago: Moody Press, n.d.

Hughes, R. Kent. *John: That You May Believe*. Preach the Word. Wheaton: Crossway Books, 1999.

Jones, Mark. *Knowing Christ*. Edinburg: Banner of Truth Trust, 2015.

Keener, Craig S. *The Bible Background Commentary*. Inter Varsity Press: Downers Grove, 1993.

Kostenberger, Andreas J. *John*. Baker Exegetical Commentary on the New Testament. Grand Rapids: Baker Books, 2004.

_____. "John," in *Zondervan Illustrated Bible Backgrounds Commentary*. Edited by Clinton E. Arnold. Grand Rapids: Zondervan, 2002.

_____. *The Theology of John's Gospels and Letters*. Grand Rapids: Zondervan, 2009.

MacArthur, John. *1 Corinthians*. MacArthur New Testament Commentary. Chicago: Moody Press, 1996.

_____. *John 1-11*. MacArthur New Testament Commentary. Chicago: Moody Press, 1006.

Milne, Bruce. *The Message of John*. Downers Grove: Inter Varsity Press, 2020.

Morris, Leon. *Reflections on the Gospel of John*. Hendrikson Publishers, Peabody, 2000.

_____. *The Gospel According to John*. Rev. ed. The New International Commentary on the New Testament. Grand Rapids: Eerdman's Publishing, 1995.

Packer, J.I. *Knowing God*. Downers Grove: Intervarsity, 1993.

Elmer, Robert. *Piercing Heaven: Prayers of the Puritans*. Bellingham: Lexham Press, 2019.

Piper, John. "God is Always Doing 1,000 Things in Your Life." Desiring God. http://www.desiring god.org/articles/god-is-always-doing-1000-things-in-your-life (accessed 8 Feb. 2022).

_____. *Spectacular Sins: And Their Global Purpose in the Glory of Christ*. Crossway Books: Wheaton, 2008.

Reymond, Robert. *A New Systematic Theology of the Christian Faith*. Thomas Nelson Publishers: Nashville, 1998.

Ryle, J.C. "St. John," in *Expository Thoughts on the Gospels*. New York: Robert Carter and Brothers, 1878.

Simeon, Charles. "Matthew." *Horae Homileticae*. London: Holdsworth and Ball, 1855.

Tenney, Merrill C. *John and Acts.* The Expositors Bible Commentary. Grand Rapids: Zondervan, 1981.

_____. *John: The Gospel of Belief.* Grand Rapids: Eerdman's Publishing, 1975.

The Westminster Shorter Catechism. Edinburg. Banner of Truth, 1998.

Tozer. A.W. *Knowledge of the Holy.* Lincoln: Back to the Bible Broadcast, 1971.

Ware, Bruce. *The Man Christ Jesus: Theological Reflections on the Humanity of Christ.* Wheaton: Crossway Books, 2012.